Baby Bibs
To Cross-Stitch

Baby Bibs to Cross-Stitch features a collection of adorable easy-to-stitch projects, perfect for anyone with limited time. All you need is a pre-finished bib and one of these designs to create handmade treasures for those special babies in your life. This book is filled with fun ideas from animals and fairies to baby sayings that everyone will love.

Produced by:

Kooler Design Studio
399 Taylor Blvd., Suite 104
Pleasant Hill, CA 94523
kds@koolerdesign.com

Production Team:
• Creative Director: Donna Kooler
• Editor-In-Chief: Judy Swager
• Technical Editor: Priscilla Timm
• Book Designer: María Parrish
• Photographers: Dianne Woods, Douglas Swager
• Photo Stylist: Basha Kooler

Published by:

Copyright ©2006 by Leisure Arts, Inc.,
104 Champs Blvd., STE 100, Maumelle, AR 72113,
www.leisurearts.com

Made in U.S.A.

i love you
BABIES are special
hot dog
GET MILK

dream
wish
you little monkey
I LOVE MOM
B IS FOR BEAUTIFUL BUBBLY BOUNCING BELOVED BABY
bon apetit!
bebe bear
bebe
baby love
veggies

Sweet Pea
SUNSHINE

Charts are in numerical order beginning on page 6.

1. Bebe Bear   **Size:** 73 x 67

X	1/4	Back	FK	DMC	Anc.	Color
				1	2	White
				322	978	Baby Blue-DK
				413	401	Pewter Gray-DK
				745	300	Yellow-LT Pale
				945	881	Tawny
				951	1010	Tawny-LT
				955	206	Nile Green-LT
				963	73	Dusty Rose-UL VY LT
				3326	36	Rose-LT
				3755	140	Baby Blue
				3823	386	Yellow-UL Pale
				3841	128	Baby Blue-Pale
				3856	367	Mahogany-UL VY LT

2. You Little Monkey **Size: 62 x 53**

X	1/4	Back	FK	DMC	Anc.	Color
			●	1	2	White
♣	♣			163	216	Celadon Green-MD
Z	Z			543	933	Beige Brown-UL VY LT
	◆	/		561	212	Jade-VY DK
■	■	/		801	359	Coffee Brown-DK
		/ *	●	801	359	Coffee Brown-DK
★	★			945	881	Tawny
⋈	⋈			951	1010	Tawny-LT
✿	✿			989	242	Forest Green
+	+			3348	264	Yellow Green-LT
♥	♥			3771	868	Terra Cotta-UL VY LT
●	●			3862	603	Mocha Beige-DK
◣	◣			3863	1084	Mocha Beige-MD
A	A			3864	831	Mocha Beige-LT

*Use 2 strands of floss

3. Bon Appétit **Size: 46 x 41**

X	1/4	Back	FK	DMC	Anc.	Color
◈	◈			1	2	White
■	◼	✎	●	310	403	Black
✛	✛			402	1047	Mahogany- VY LT
♥	♥	✎	●	606	334	Bright Orange-Red
H	H			945	881	Tawny
◩	◩			3064	883	Desert Sand
Z	Z			3326	36	Rose-LT
↑	↑			3755	140	Baby Blue
✳				3771	868	Terra Cotta-UL VY LT
◆	◆			3776	1048	Mahogany-LT
▣	▣			3841	128	Baby Blue-Pale

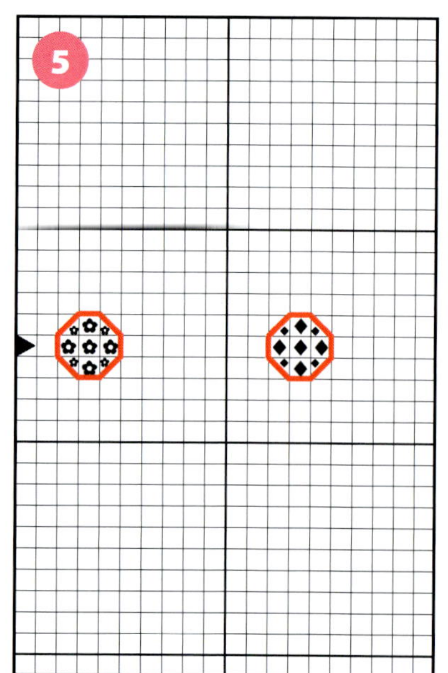

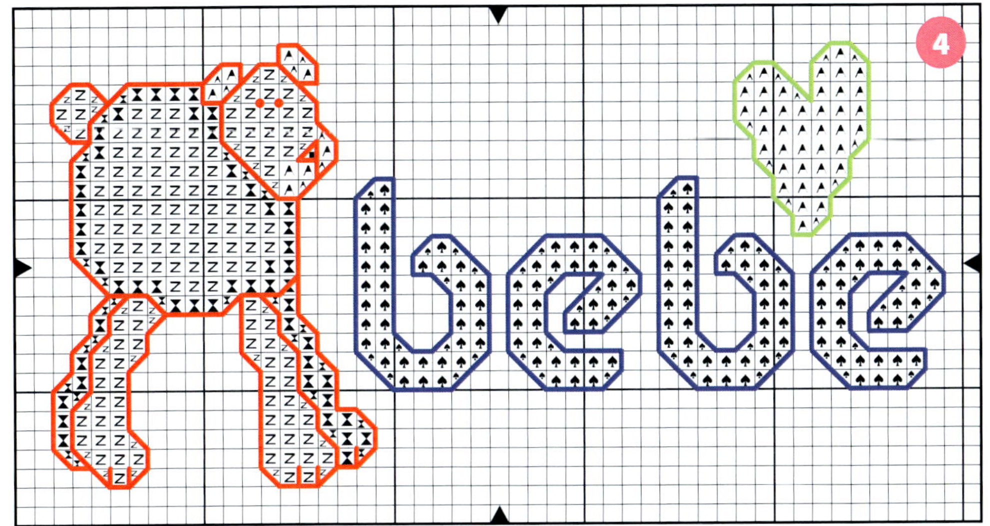

4. Bebe   **Size:** 47 x 23

X	1/4	Back	FK	DMC	Anc.	Color
		✎		322	978	Baby Blue-DK
■		✎	●	801	359	Coffee Brown-DK
		✎		899	52	Rose-MD
A	A			963	73	Dusty Rose-UL VY LT
X	X			3064	883	Desert Sand
♠	♠			3755	140	Baby Blue
Z	Z			3771	868	Terra Cotta-UL VY LT

5. Bunny   **Size:** 88 x 27

X	1/4	Back	FK	DMC	Anc.	Color
◈	◈			1	2	White
■	■			210	108	Lavender-MD
		✎		334	977	Baby Blue-MD
X	X	✎		352	9	Coral-LT
↑	↑			745	300	Yellow-LT Pale
H	H			775	128	Baby Blue-VY LT
		✎	●	801	359	Coffee Brown-DK
×	×			945	881	Tawny
Z	Z			951	1010	Tawny-LT
✿	✿			955	206	Nile Green-LT
◆	◆			963	73	Dusty Rose-UL VY LT
♥	♥			3326	36	Rose-LT
✳	✳			3823	386	Yellow-UL Pale
◤	◤			3856	367	Mahogany-UL VY LT

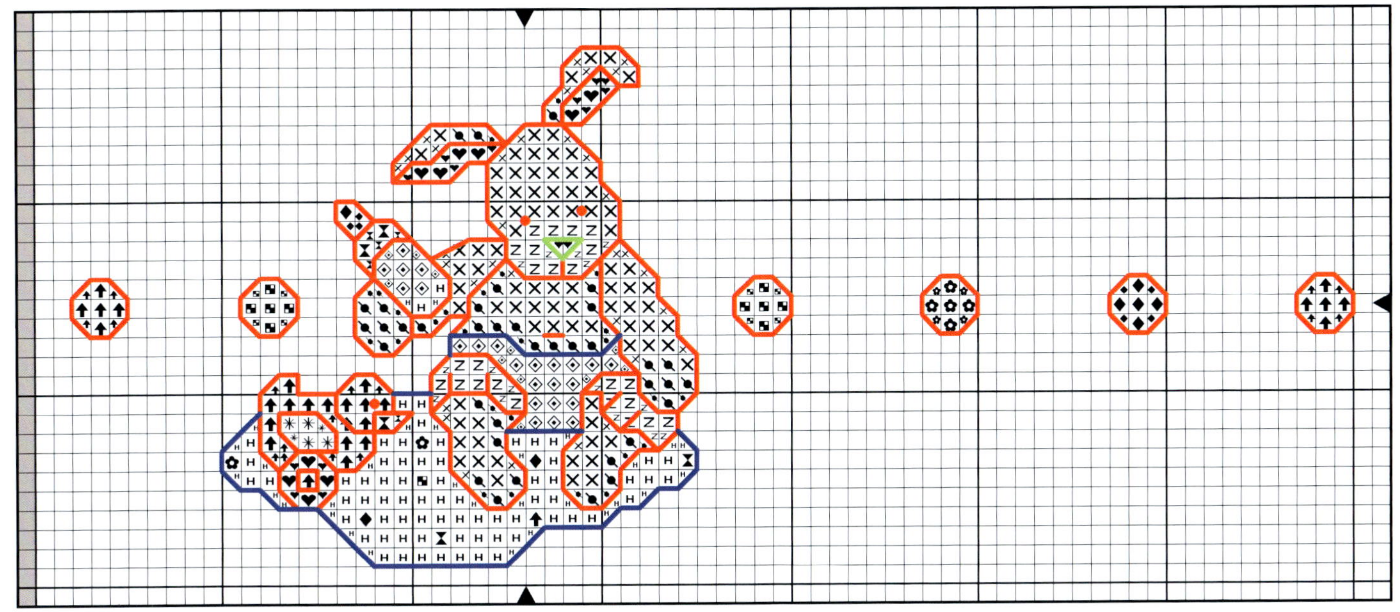

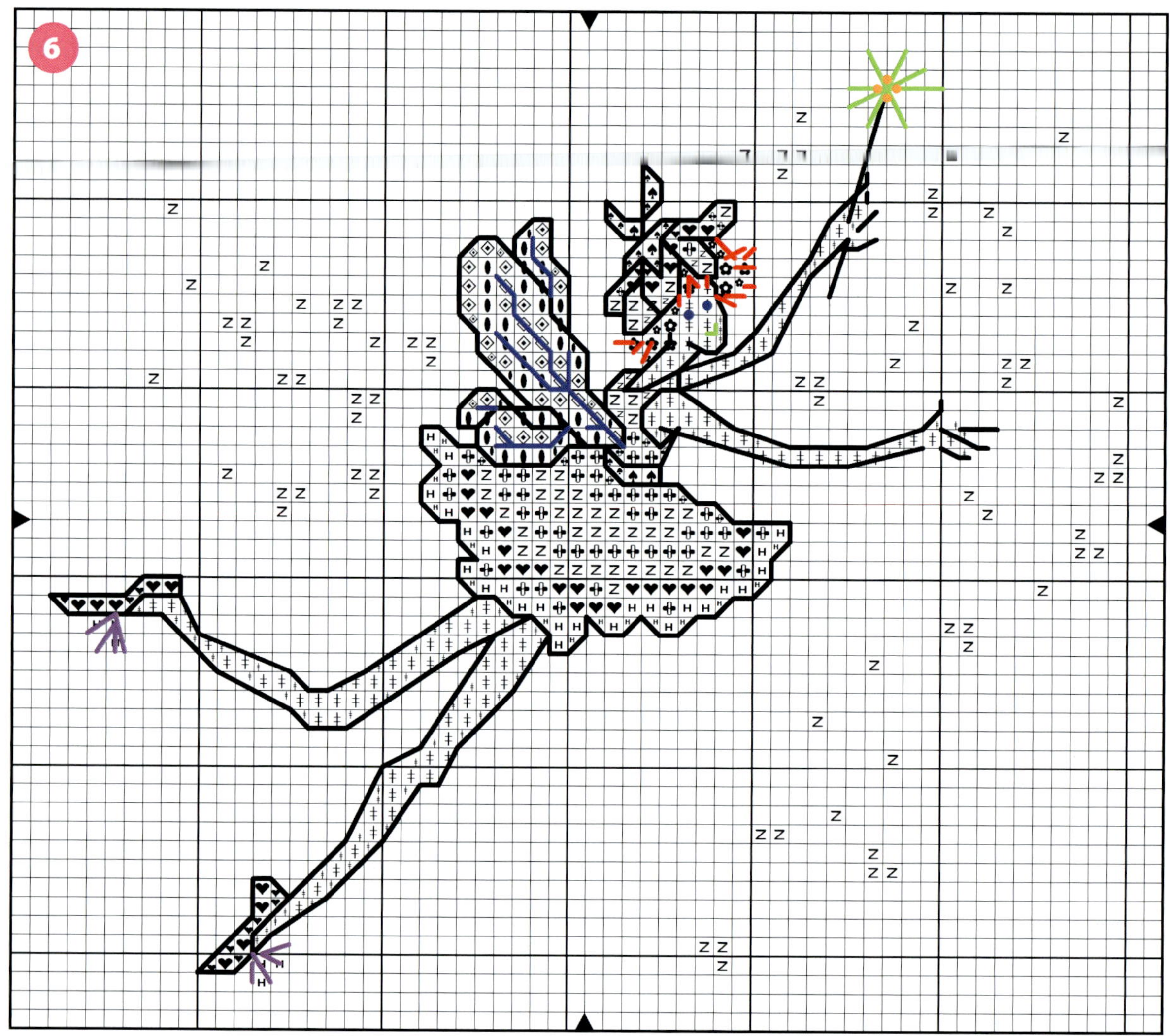

6. Fairy **Size:** 58 x 50

X	1/4	Back	FK	DMC	Anc.	Color
◈	◈			1	2	White
		✎		209	109	Lavender-DK
H	H			211	342	Lavender-LT
		✎	●	413	401	Pewter Gray-DK
♥	♥	✎		603	62	Cranberry
✛	✛			604	55	Cranberry-LT
Z	Z		●	605	50	Cranberry-VY LT
		✎		721	324	Orange Spice-MD
✿	✿			722	323	Orange Spice-LT
‡	‡			945	881	Tawny
♠	♠			3348	264	Yellow Green LT
		✎		3755	140	Baby Blue
❙	❙			3756	1037	Baby Blue-UL VY LT

7. Giraffes   Size: 49 x 48

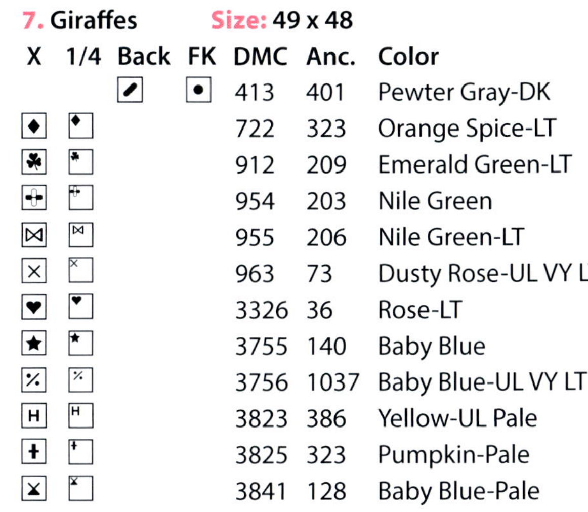

X   1/4   Back   FK   DMC   Anc.   Color
                   413   401   Pewter Gray-DK
                   722   323   Orange Spice-LT
                   912   209   Emerald Green-LT
                   954   203   Nile Green
                   955   206   Nile Green-LT
                   963   73   Dusty Rose-UL VY LT
                   3326 36   Rose-LT
                   3755 140   Baby Blue
                   3756 1037   Baby Blue-UL VY LT
                   3823 386   Yellow-UL Pale
                   3825 323   Pumpkin-Pale
                   3841 128   Baby Blue-Pale

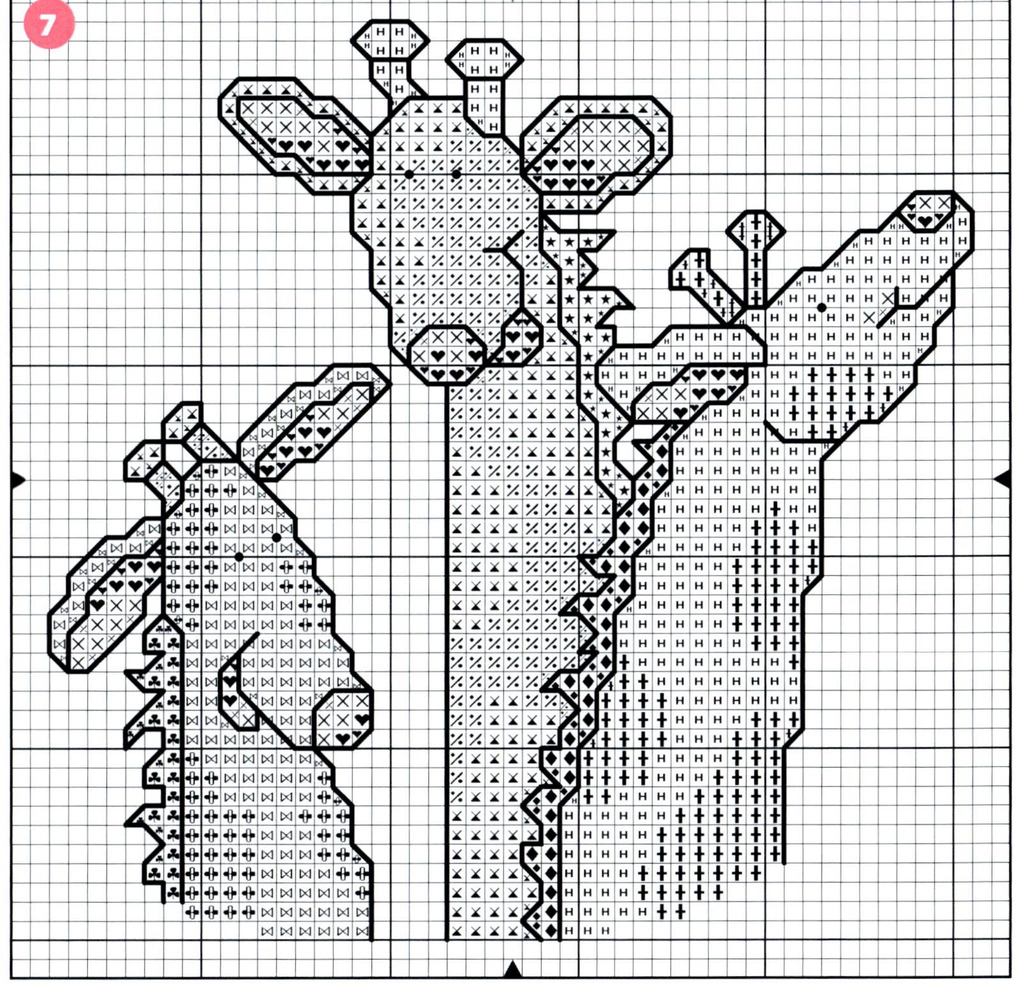

8. Sunshine Size: 94 x 29

X	1/4	Back	FK	DMC	Anc.	Color
				745	300	Yellow-LT Pale
				746	275	Off White
				801	359	Coffee Brown-DK
		*		801	359	Coffee Brown-DK
				818	23	Baby Pink
				899	52	Rose-MD
				3326	36	Rose-LT
				3853	1003	Autumn Gold-DK
				3854	1047	Autumn Gold-MD
				3855	361	Autumn Gold-LT

* Use 2 strands of floss

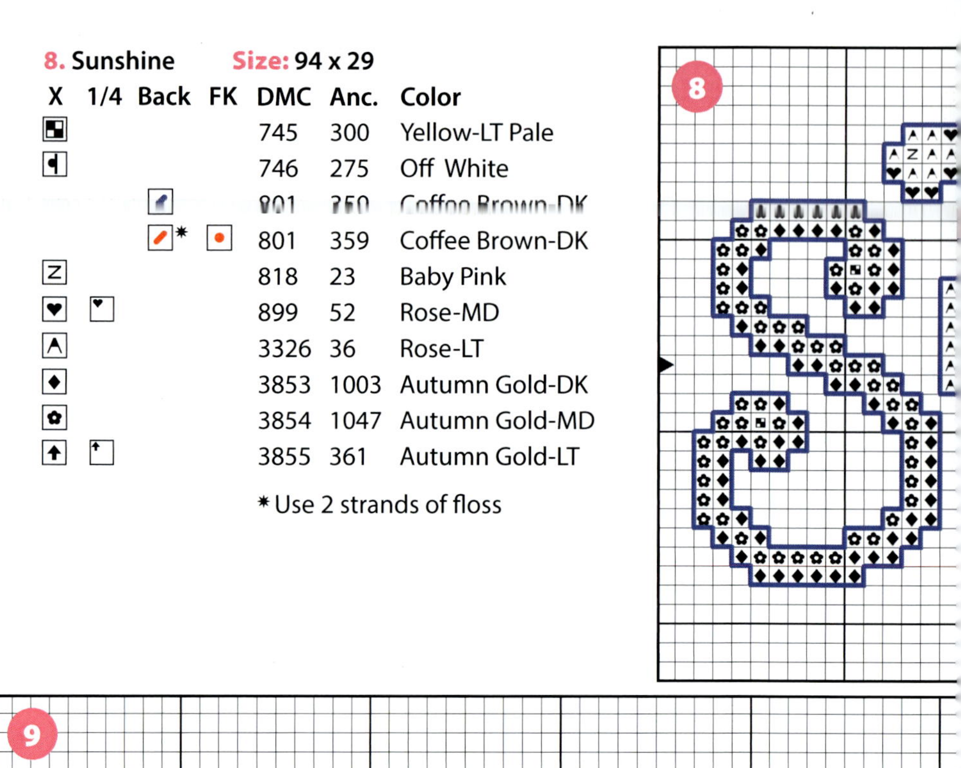

9. Fishies Size: 108 x 29

X	1/4	Back	DMC	Anc.	Color
			1	2	White
			322	978	Baby Blue-DK
			351	10	Coral
			352	9	Coral-LT
			353	6	Peach
			413	401	Pewter Gray-DK
			436	1045	Tan
			738	361	Tan-VY LT
			743	302	Yellow-MD
			744	301	Yellow-Pale
			745	300	Yellow-LT Pale
			775	128	Baby Blue-VY LT
			912	209	Emerald Green-LT
			954	203	Nile Green
			955	206	Nile Green-LT
			975	355	Golden Brown-DK
			3326	36	Rose-LT
			3755	140	Baby Blue
			3841	128	Baby Blue-Pale

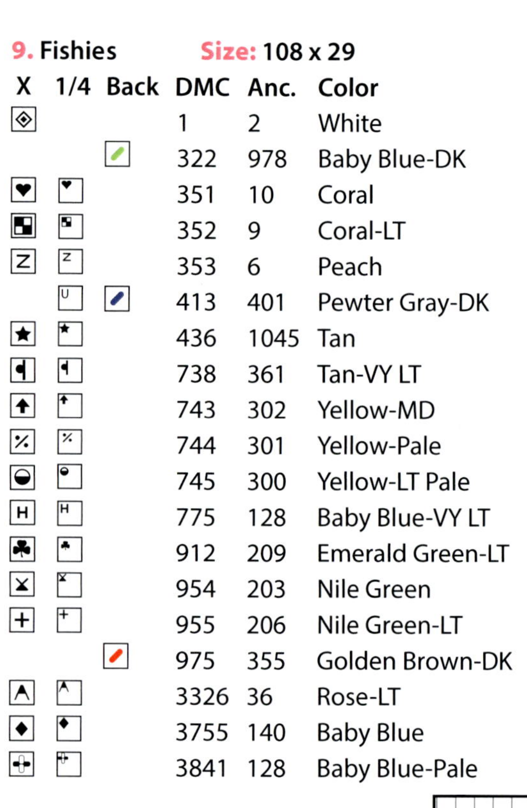

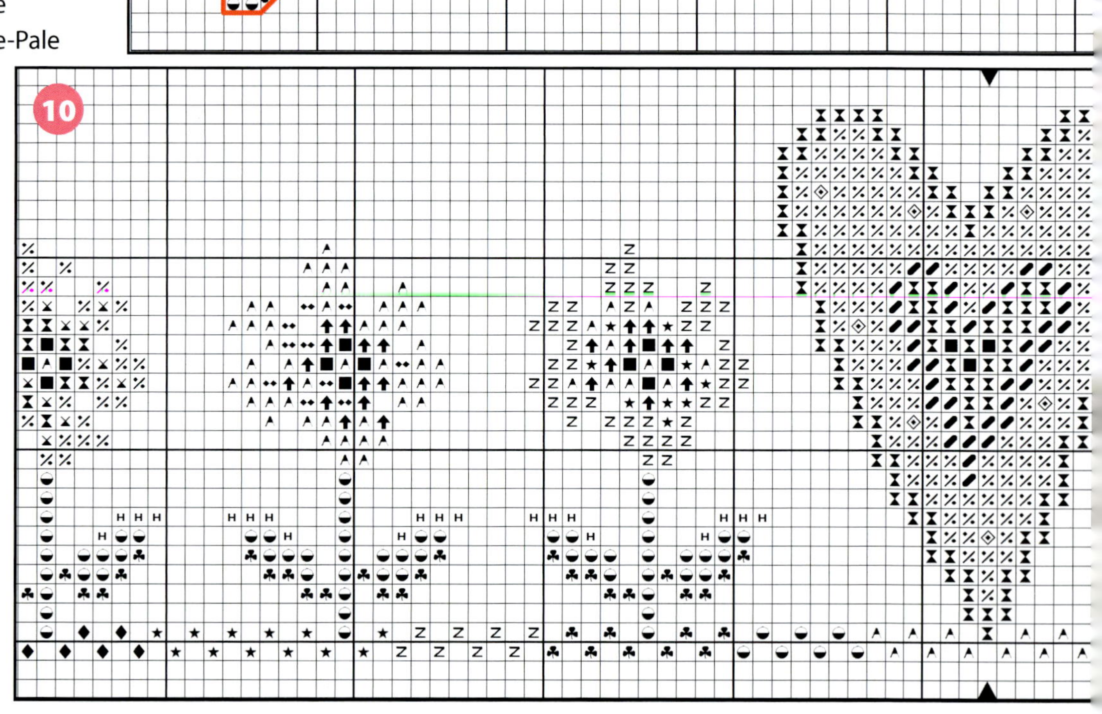

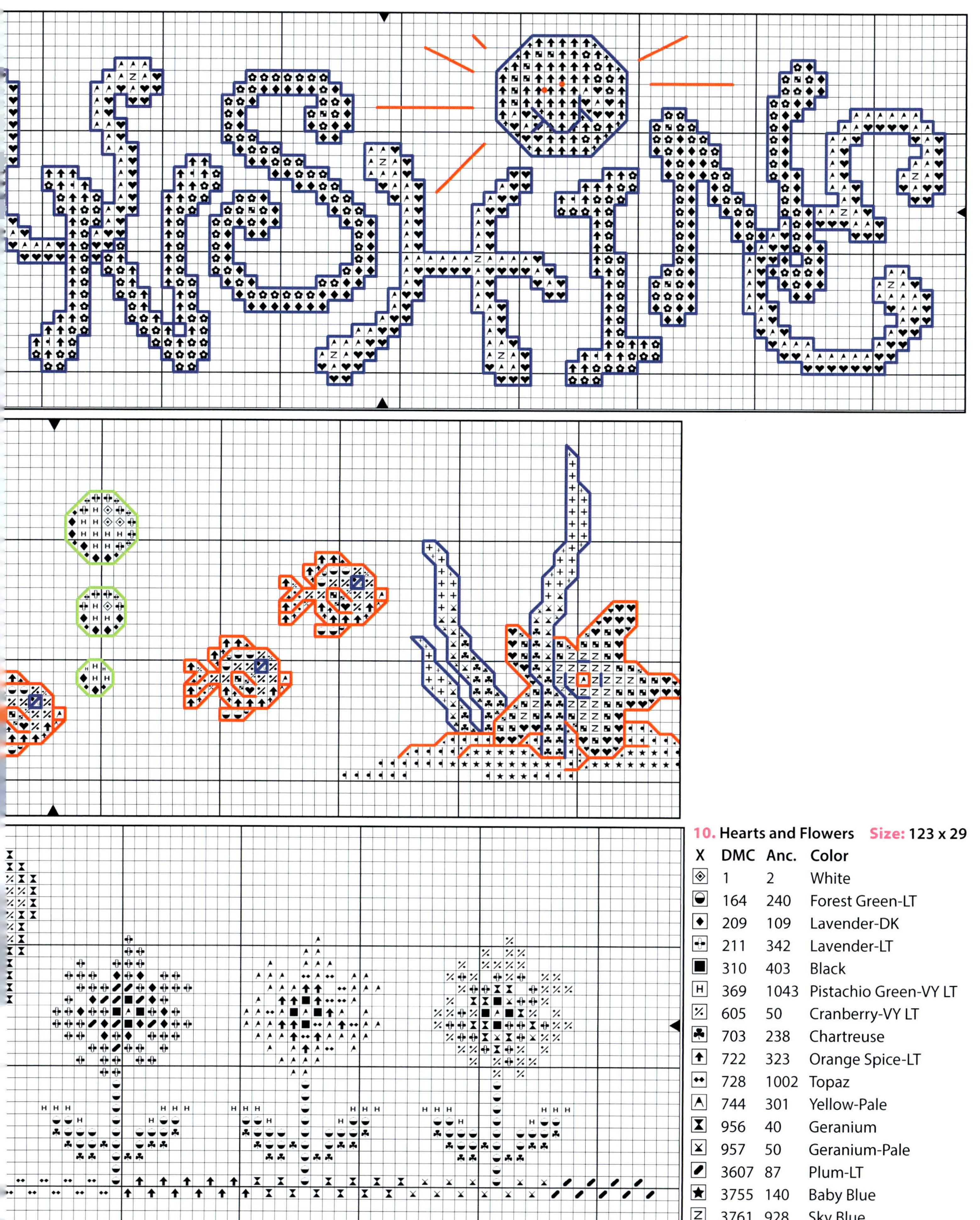

10. Hearts and Flowers **Size:** 123 x 29

X	DMC	Anc.	Color
◈	1	2	White
◉	164	240	Forest Green-LT
◆	209	109	Lavender-DK
⊞	211	342	Lavender-LT
■	310	403	Black
H	369	1043	Pistachio Green-VY LT
⅔	605	50	Cranberry-VY LT
♣	703	238	Chartreuse
↑	722	323	Orange Spice-LT
••	728	1002	Topaz
A	744	301	Yellow-Pale
✕	956	40	Geranium
✕	957	50	Geranium-Pale
✦	3607	87	Plum-LT
★	3755	140	Baby Blue
Z	3761	928	Sky Blue

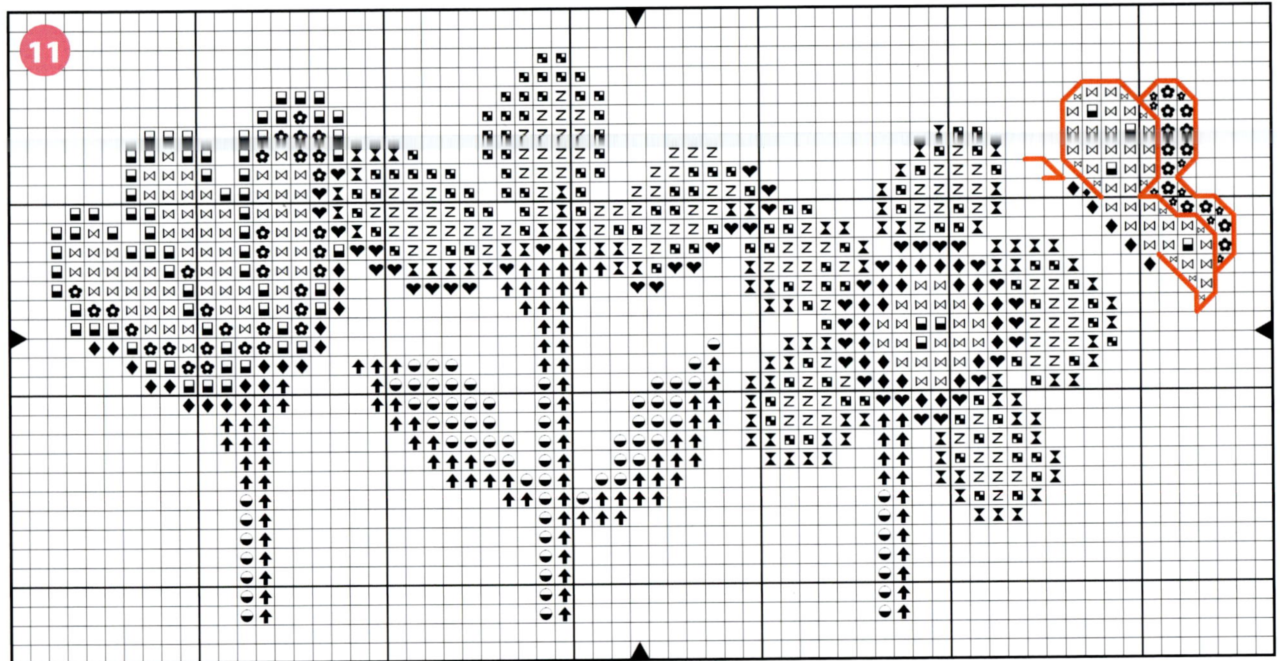

11. Flowers   **Size:** 63 x 30

X	1/4	Back	DMC	Anc.	Color
♥			335	38	Rose
▣			604	55	Cranberry-LT
Z			605	50	Cranberry-VY LT
◆	◆	╱	721	324	Orange Spice-MD
▣			722	323	Orange Spice-LT
⋈	⋈		745	300	Yellow-LT Pale
⧗			899	52	Rose-MD
↑			912	209	Emerald Green-LT
◗			954	203	Nile Green
✿	✿		3825	323	Pumpkin-Pale

12. Elephant   **Size:** 59 x 55

X	1/4	Back	FK	DMC	Anc.	Color
◈	◈			1	2	White
		✎	●	413	401	Pewter Gray-DK
◆	◆			744	301	Yellow-Pale
◖	◖			745	300	Yellow-LT Pale
◧	◧			775	128	Baby Blue-VY LT
✕	✕			963	73	Dusty Rose-UL VY LT
♥	♥			3326	36	Rose-LT
⊠	⊠			3841	128	Baby Blue-Pale

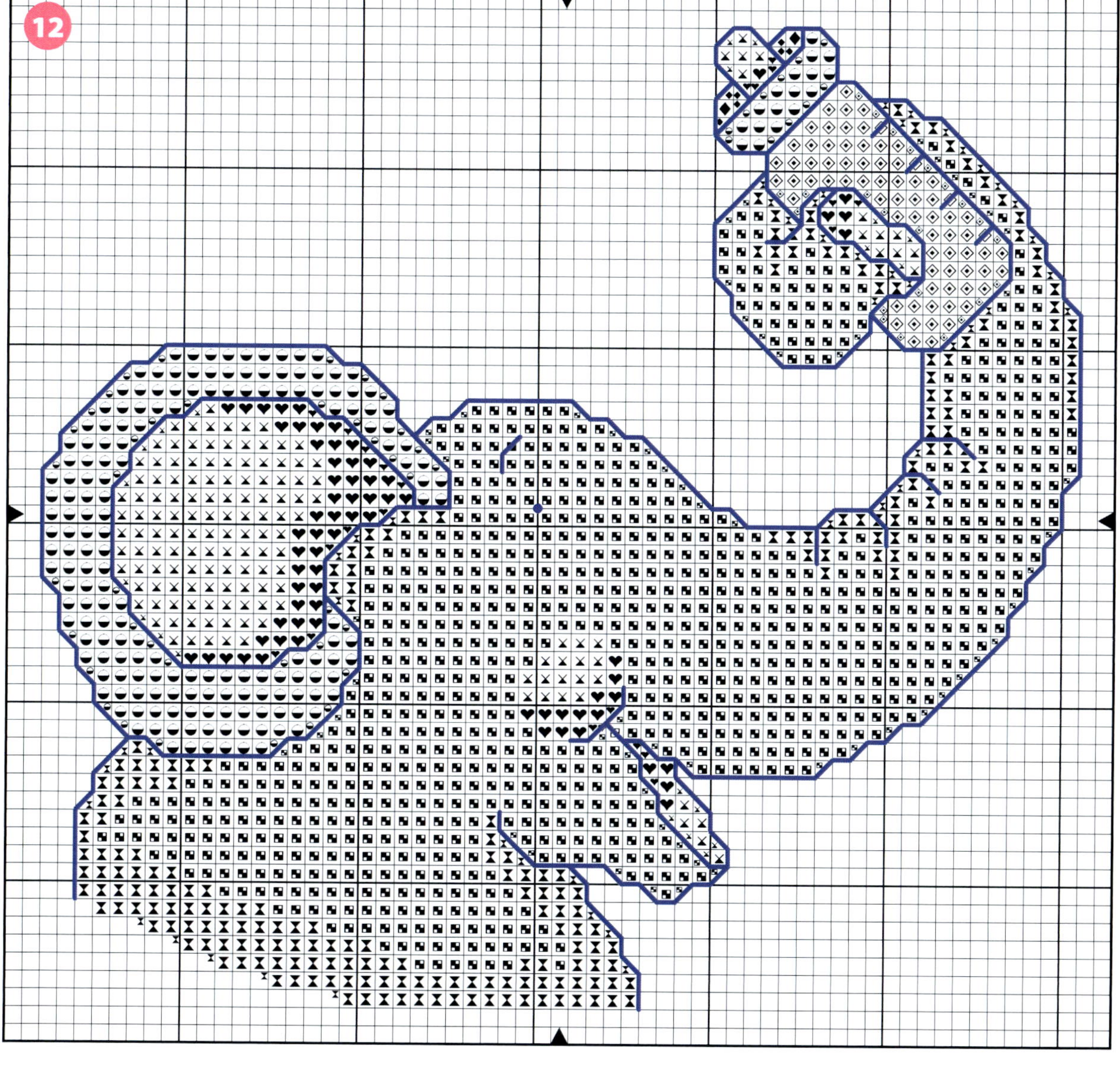

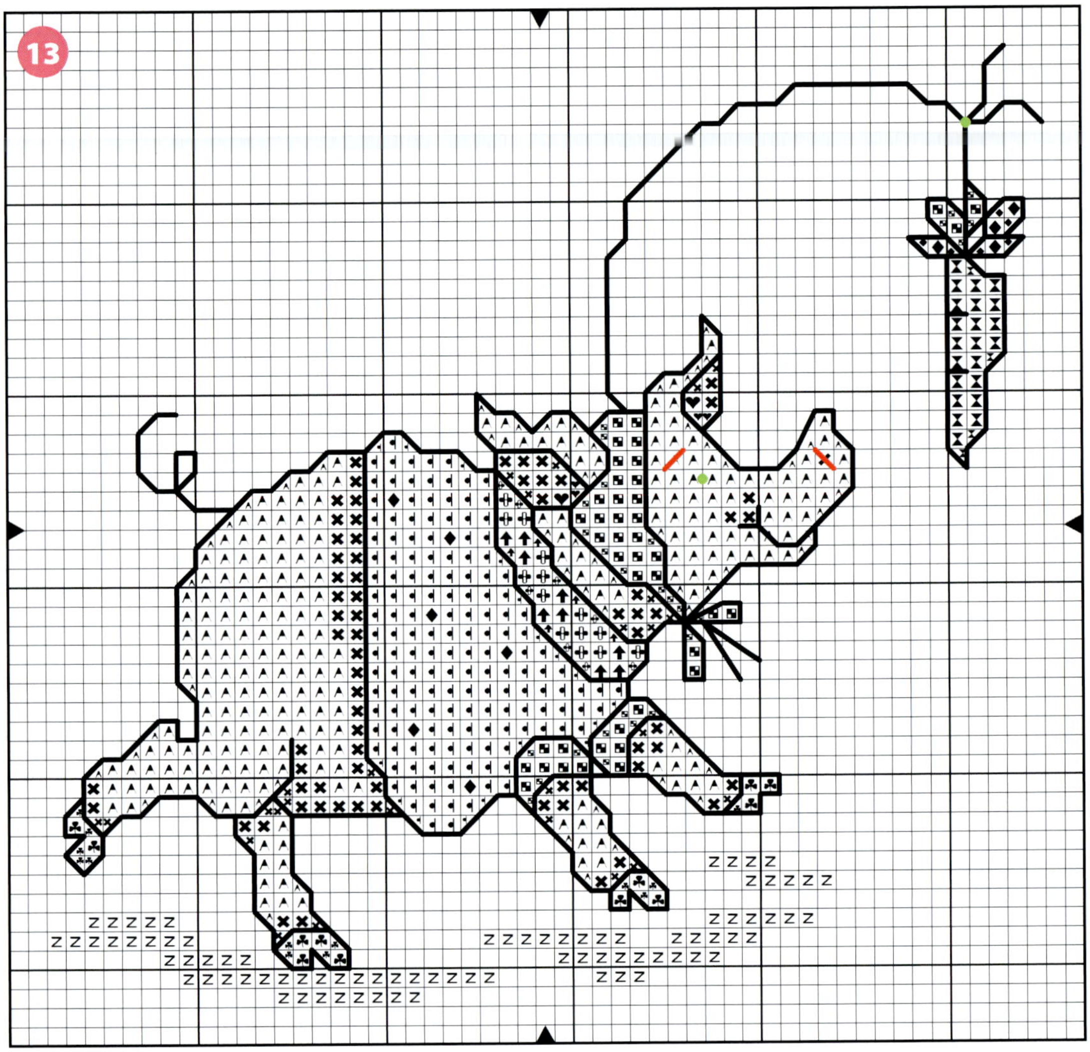

13

13. Piggy   **Size:** 53 x 50

X	1/4	Back	FK	DMC	Anc.	Color
♥	♥	/		335	38	Rose
		/	•	413	401	Pewter Gray-DK
♣	♣			415	398	Pearl Gray
✚	✚			745	300	Yellow-LT Pale
◼	◼			772	259	Yellow Green-VY LT
▲	▲			963	73	Dusty Rose-UL VY LT
✖	✖			3326	36	Rose-LT
◆	◆			3348	264	Yellow Green-LT
Z	Z			3756	1037	Baby Blue-UL VY LT
◀	◀			3823	386	Yellow-UL Pale
⊠	⊠			3825	323	Pumpkin-Pale
↑	↑			3841	128	Baby Blue-Pale

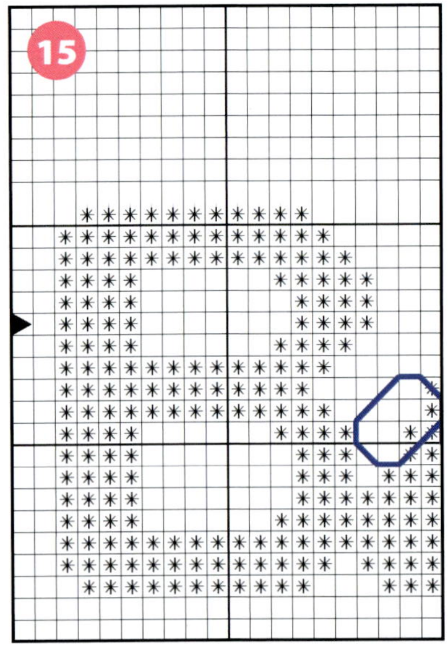

14. Dream   **Size:** 42 x 21

X	1/4	Back	DMC	Anc.	Color
♠	♠		209	109	Lavender-DK
◇	◇		211	342	Lavender-LT
♥	♥		351	10	Coral
⊠	⊠		352	9	Coral-LT
Z	Z		353	6	Peach
■		✎	413	401	Pewter Gray-DK
◆	◆		604	55	Cranberry-LT
✳	✳		605	50	Cranberry-VY LT
◉	◉		745	300	Yellow-LT Pale
H	H		775	128	Baby Blue-VY LT
		✎	912	209	Emerald Green-LT
♣	♣		954	203	Nile Green
◣	◣		3755	140	Baby Blue
★	★		3855	361	Autumn Gold-LT

15. Babies Are Special   **Size:** 81 x 25

X	1/4	Back	DMC	Anc.	Color
		✎	322	978	Baby Blue-DK
✳			955	206	Nile Green-LT
Z			963	73	Dusty Rose-UL VY LT
♥			3326	36	Rose-LT

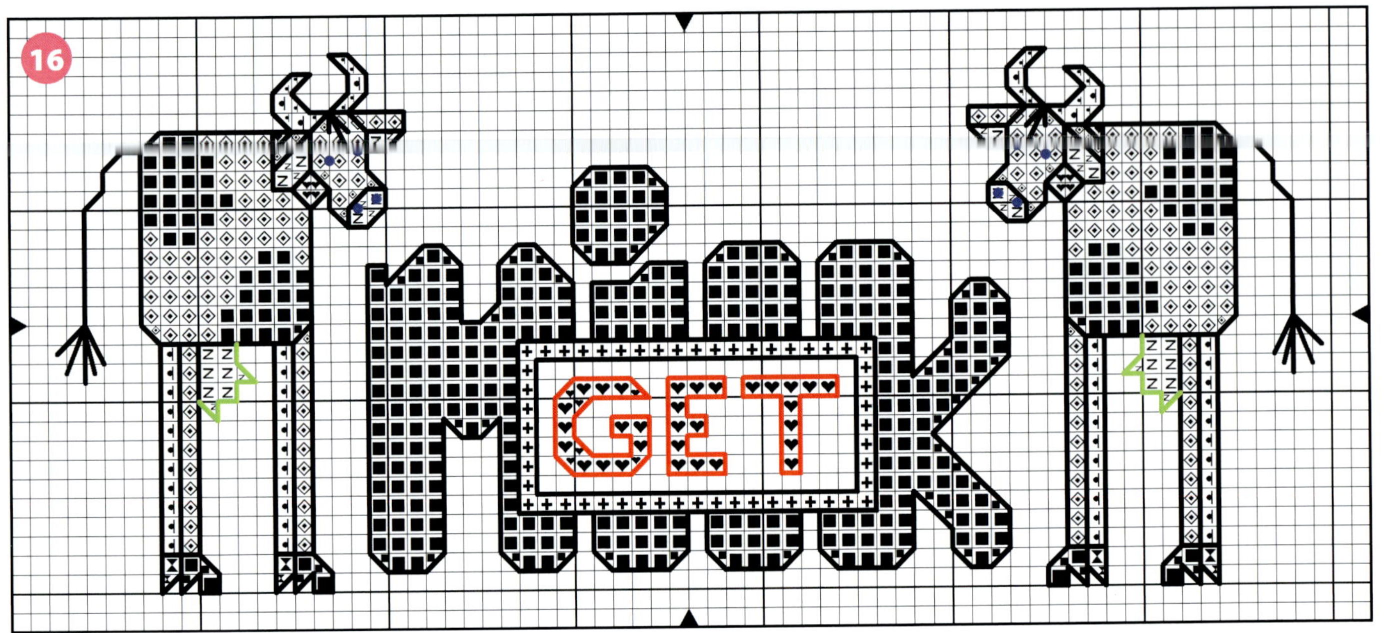

16. Get Milk   **Size:** 68 x 28

X	1/4	Back	FK	DMC	Anc.	Color
◈	◈			1	2	White
■	■	✏	•	310	403	Black
✗	✗	✏		414	235	Steel Gray-DK
◀	◀			415	398	Pearl Gray
♥	♥	✏		606	334	Bright Orange-Red
✚				744	301	Yellow-Pale
Z	Z			776	24	Pink-MD

18. I Love Veggies   **Size:** 47 x 27

X	1/4	Back	FK	DMC	Anc.	Color
♥	♥			352	9	Coral-LT
H	H			353	6	Peach
		✏	•	413	401	Pewter Gray-DK
♣	♣			772	259	Yellow Green-VY LT
Z	Z			818	23	Baby Pink

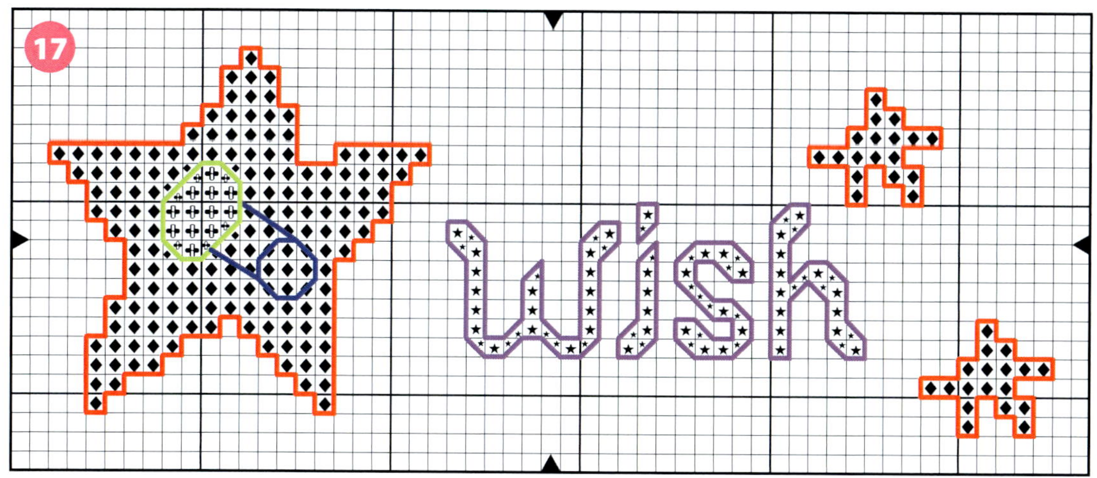

17. Wish   **Size:** 53 x 20

X	1/4	Back	DMC	Anc.	Color
		✏	209	109	Lavender-DK
★	★		210	108	Lavender-MD
		✏	334	977	Baby Blue-MD
		✏	728	1002	Topaz
◆	◆		745	300	Yellow-LT Pale
		✏	912	209	Emerald Green-LT
⊞	⊞		955	206	Nile Green-LT

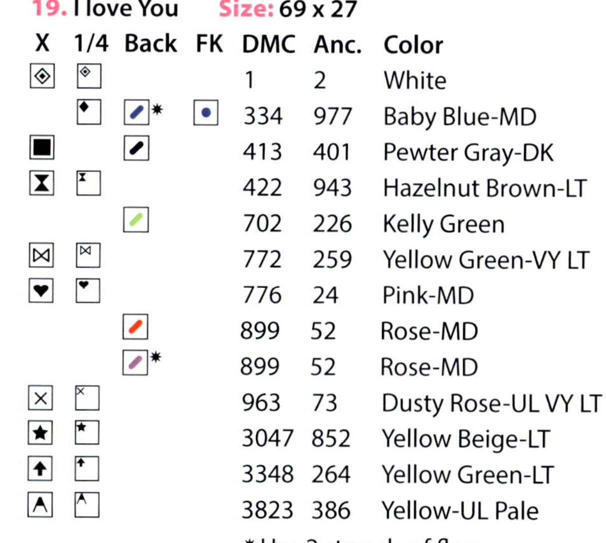

19. I love You   **Size:** 69 x 27

X	1/4	Back	FK	DMC	Anc.	Color
◈	◈			1	2	White
	◆	✏*	●	334	977	Baby Blue-MD
■		✏		413	401	Pewter Gray-DK
⚟	⚟			422	943	Hazelnut Brown-LT
		✏		702	226	Kelly Green
⋈	⋈			772	259	Yellow Green-VY LT
♥	♥			776	24	Pink-MD
		✏		899	52	Rose-MD
		✏*		899	52	Rose-MD
✕	✕			963	73	Dusty Rose-UL VY LT
★	★			3047	852	Yellow Beige-LT
↑	↑			3348	264	Yellow Green-LT
⋀	⋀			3823	386	Yellow-UL Pale

* Use 2 strands of floss

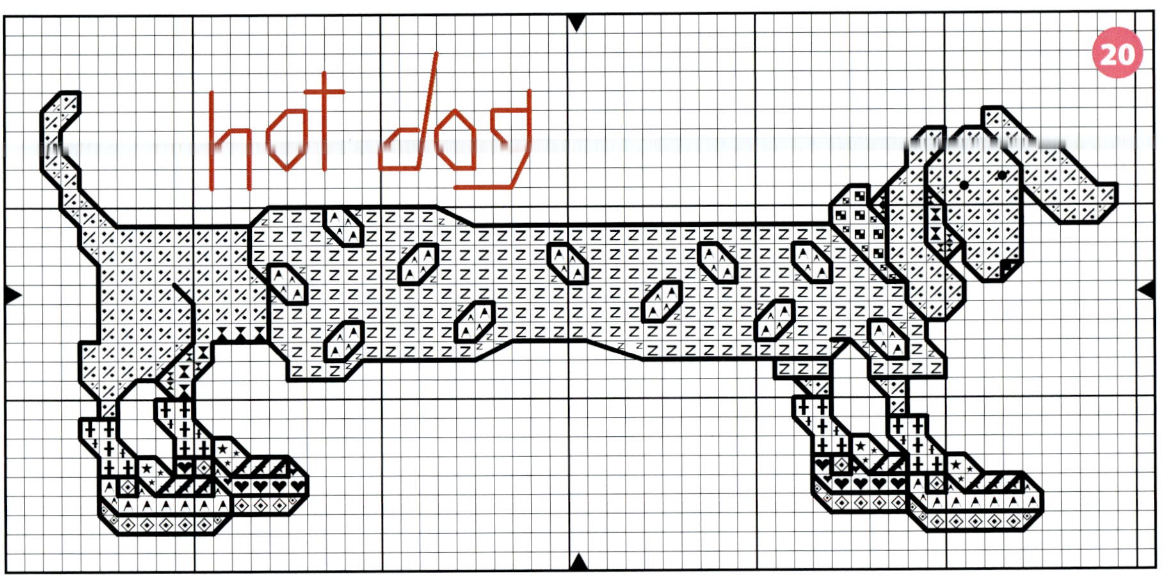

20. Hot Dog   **Size:** 57 x 25

X	1/4	Back	FK	DMC	Anc.	Color
◈	◈			1	2	White
★	★			210	108	Lavender-MD
◪	◪			334	977	Baby Blue-MD
◼	◼	✎	●	413	401	Pewter Gray-DK
⋀	⋀			606	334	Bright Orange-Red
✚	✚			703	238	Chartreuse
Z	Z			745	300	Yellow-LT Pale
♥	♥	✎		817	13	Coral-Red-VY DK
⊠	⊠			3064	883	Desert Sand
⁒	⁒			3771	868	Terra Cotta-UL VY LT

21. Sweet Pea   **Size:** 82 x 30

X	1/4	Back	FK	DMC	Anc.	Color
◆	◆	✎	●	561	212	Jade-VY DK
		✎*		561	212	Jade-VY DK
◧				563	208	Jade-LT
♥	♥			760	1022	Salmon
Z				761	1021	Salmon-LT
⋀	⋀			772	259	Yellow Green-VY LT
		✎*		988	243	Forest Green- MD
⊠	⊠			989	242	Forest Green
⋈	⋈			3348	264	Yellow Green-LT
◖	◖			3815	877	Celadon Green-DK
◣	◣			3816	876	Celadon Green-MD

*Use 2 strands of floss

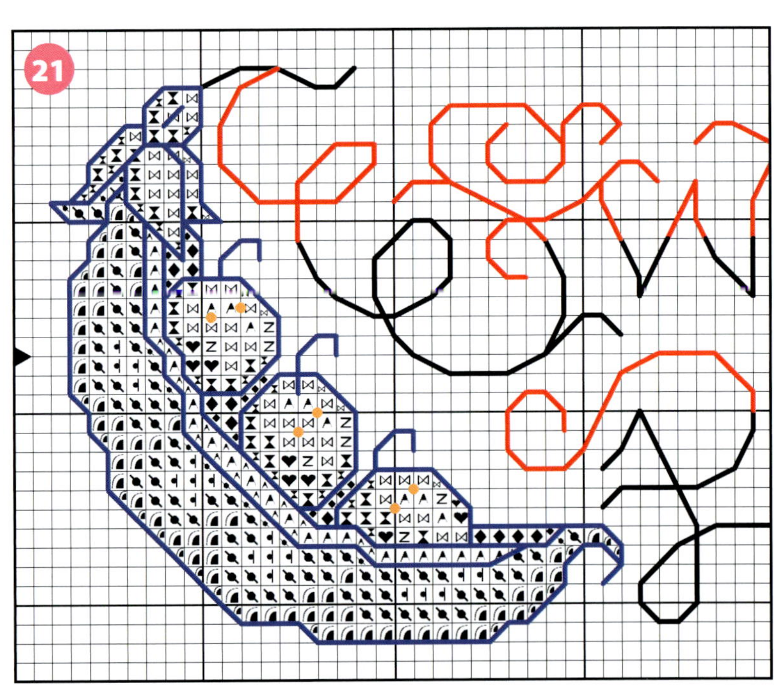

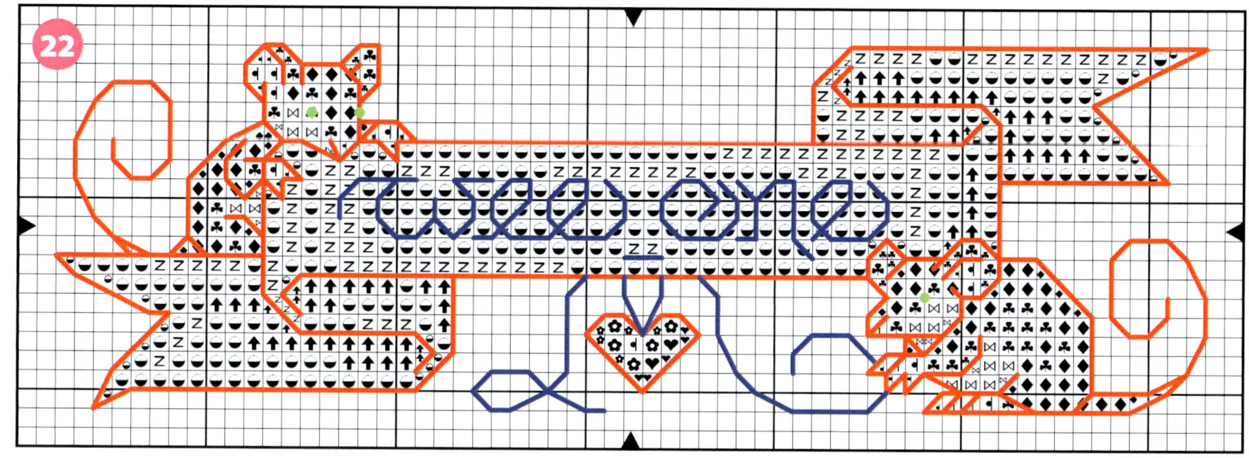

22. Wee One   **Size:** 61 x 19

X	1/4	Back	FK	DMC	Anc.	Color
♥	♥			335	38	Rose
		✒		505	210	Jade
Z	z			745	300	Yellow-LT Pale
⋈	⋈			746	275	Off White
◗	◗			761	1021	Salmon-LT
		◢	●	801	359	Coffee Brown-DK
✿	✿			899	52	Rose-MD
↑	↑			3854	1047	Autumn Gold-MD
◖	◖			3855	361	Autumn Gold-LT
◆	◆			3863	1084	Mocha Beige-MD
♣	♣			3864	831	Mocha Beige-LT

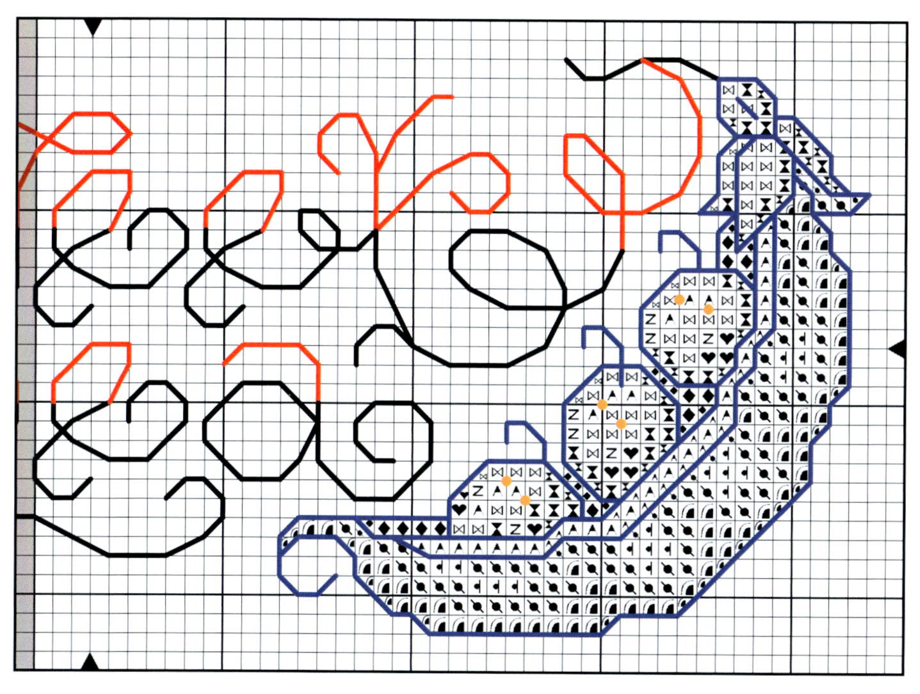

23. B is for Baby **Size:** 55 x 46

X	1/4	Back	FK	DMC	Anc.	Color
♥	♥	╱	●	335	38	Rose
↑				340	118	Blue Violet-MD
Z	Z			899	52	Rose-MD
◬	◬	╱		3347	266	Yellow Green-MD
⊥				3811	928	Turquoise-VY LT
✖	✕	╱		3815	877	Celadon Green-DK
$	$			3816	876	Celadon Green-MD
◆	◆			3854	1047	Autumn Gold-MD
+	+			3855	361	Autumn Gold-LT

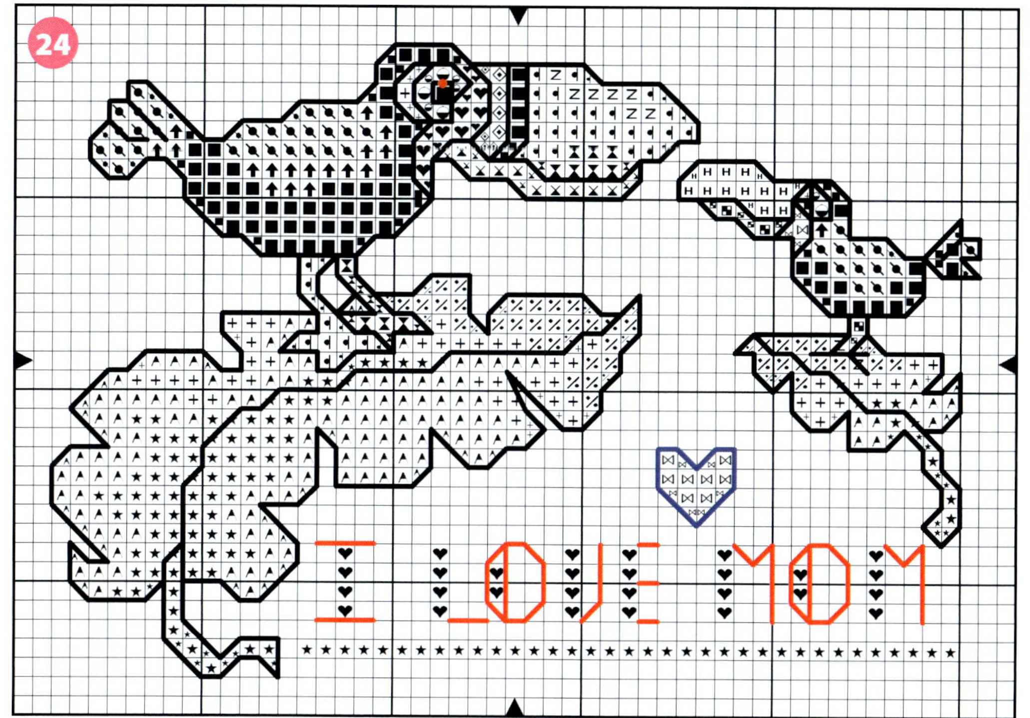

24. I Love Mom   Size: 49 x 33

X	1/4	Back	FK	DMC	Anc.	Color
◈	◈		●	1	2	White
■	■	✎		310	403	Black
▧	▧			352	9	Coral-LT
H	H			353	6	Peach
⬆		✎		413	401	Pewter Gray-DK
◤	◤			414	235	Steel Gray-DK
⋈	⋈			603	62	Cranberry
♥	♥	✎		606	334	Bright Orange-Red
★	★			701	227	Christmas Green-LT
▲	▲			703	238	Chartreuse
✚	✚			704	256	Chartreuse-BRT
⧖	⧖			721	324	Orange Spice-MD
◀	◀			722	323	Orange Spice-LT
◖	◖			743	302	Yellow-MD
⁒	⁒			772	259	Yellow Green-VY LT
✖	✖			3340	329	Apricot-MD
Z	Z			3825	323	Pumpkin-Pale

25. Baby Love   Size: 60 x 15

X	1/4	Back	DMC	Anc.	Color
		✎	322	978	Baby Blue-DK
		✎	899	206	Rose-MD
♥	♥		963	73	Dusty Rose-UL VY LT
⬆	⬆		3841	128	Baby Blue-Pale

General Instructions

Working With Charts

How To Read Charts: Each chart is made up of a key and a gridded design on which each square represents a stitch. The symbols in the key tell which floss color to use for each stitch in the chart. The following headings and symbols are given:

X — Cross Stitch
1/4 — Quarter Stitch
Back — Backstitch
DMC — DMC color number
Anc. — Anchor color number
Color — The name given to the floss color in these charts.

 A square filled with a symbol should be worked as a **Cross Stitch**.

 A triangle with a reduced symbol should be worked as a **Quarter Stitch**.

 A straight line should be worked as a **Backstitch**.

Sometimes the symbol for a **Cross Stitch** may be partially covered when a **Backstitch** crosses the square.

✻ Models were stitched using 3 strands of floss for Cross-Stitch. Use 1 or 2 strands for Backstitching and 1 strand for French Knots, as indicated in key.

Stitch Diagrams

Counted Cross-Stitch (X): Work one Cross-Stitch to correspond to each symbol on the chart. For horizontal rows, work stitches in two journeys (Fig. 1). For vertical rows, complete each stitch as shown (Fig. 2).

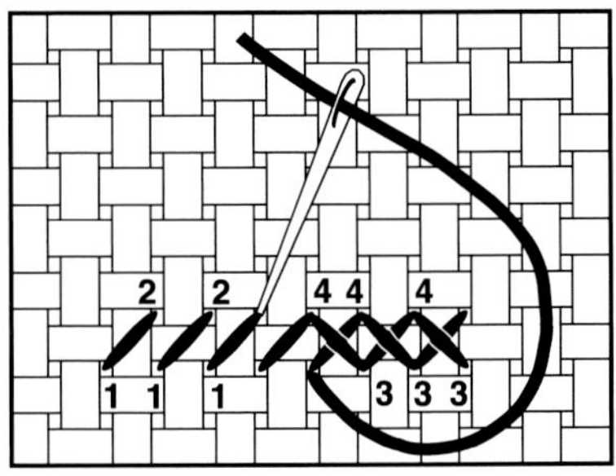

Fig. 1   Fig. 2

When the chart shows a Backstitch crossing a symbol (Fig. 3), a Cross-Stitch (Fig. 1 or 2) should be worked first, then the Backstitch (Fig. 5) should be worked on top of the Cross-Stitch.

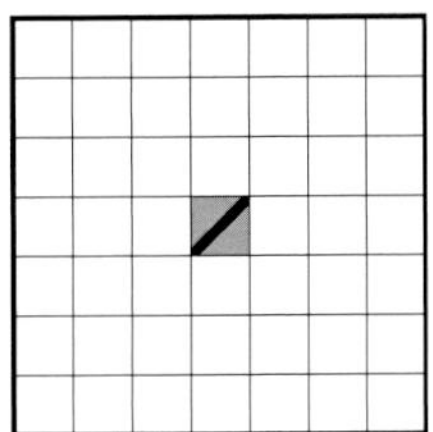

Fig. 3

Quarter Stitch (1/4): Quarter Stitches are denoted by a reduced symbol on the chart and on the color key. Come up at 1, then split fabric thread to go down at 2 (Fig. 4).

Fig. 4

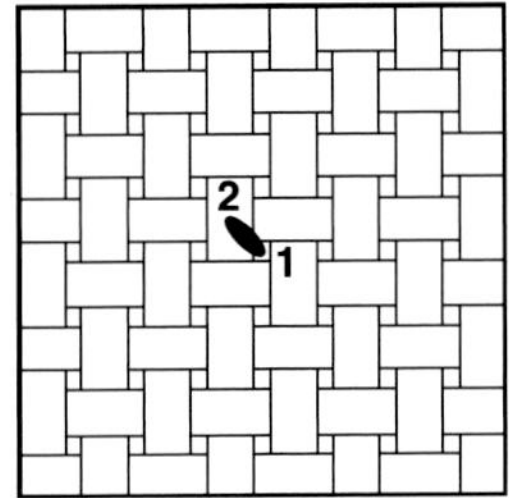

Backstitch (Back): For outline detail, Backstitch (shown on chart and on color key by colored straight lines) should be worked after the design has been completed (Fig. 5).

Fig. 5

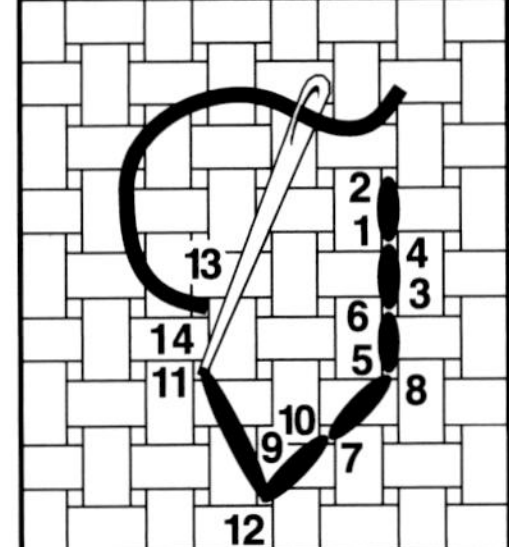

French Knot (FK): Bring needle up at 1. Wrap floss once around needle and insert needle at 2, holding end of floss with non-stitching fingers (Fig. 6). Tighten knot, then pull needle through fabric, holding floss until it must be released. For larger knot, use more strands; wrap only once.

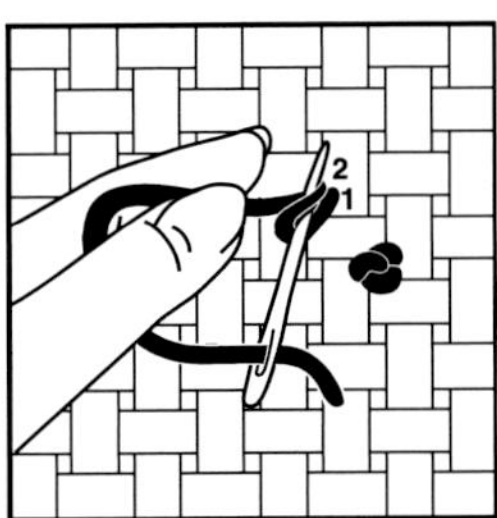

Fig. 6